Hymns of the Early Church

By Rev. John Brownlie, D.D.

This Edition Edited by Anthony Uyl

Devoted Publishing

Woodstock, Ontario, Canada 2018

Hymns of the Early Church
By Rev. John Brownlie, D.D.
This Edition Edited by Anthony Uyl

Translated from Greek and Latin Sources; Together with Translations from a Later Period; Centos and Suggestions from the Greek; and Several Original Pieces

What kind of philosophies do you have?
Let us know!

Visit our website: www.devotedpublishing.com
Contact us at: devotedpub@hotmail.com
Visit us on Facebook: @DevotedPublishing

Published in Woodstock, Ontario, Canada 2018.

For bulk educational rates, please contact us at the above email address.

ISBN: 978-1-77356-244-5

Table of Contents

Hymns of the Early Church

HYMNS OF THE EARLY CHURCH

1. Morning

Wake, awake to duty!
See, the morning light
Falls with radiant beauty
From the arms of night.
Claim the hours before thee
For the tasks of life,
Thousand calls implore thee
From the din of strife.

Listless minds are dreaming,
Idle hands are still;
Evil hearts are scheming
Purposes of ill.
See the hands that beckon,
Hear the call of right;
Thou with God must reckon
Up, and toil and fight!

Through the hours of morning,
At the height of noon,
When the light gives warning
Night approaches soon:
Do the task with gladness
Which the hours present;
Who can tell the sadness
Of a day mis-spent?

Day by day declineth,
Time is getting hoar;
Soon yon sun that shineth
Sets for evermore.
Ah, the City glorious,
Where they need no sun,
Ah, the band victorious,
And the glad "Well done"!

2.

Thine be the glory, God of Light,
For all the joy from morn that springs;
Oh, may a morn dispel each night,
And bless our lives with beauteous things.

Give us this day the light that dwells
In every heart Thy presence fills;
That night with all its fears dispels,
And life, and hope, and joy instils.

Then shall our nights no darkness bring,
But morn, bright morn, for ever shine;
And when night spreads her dusky wings,
More bright shall be the light Divine.

All praise to Thee, the God of Light;
All praise to Christ, the glorious Son;
And to the Spirit, Lord of might,
Now, and while endless ages run.

3.

With beauty decked the morn ascends,
And all the earth is bright;
And lo, the sun the darkness rends,
And floods the sky with light.

All hail, Thou Sun of Righteousness,
Upon our night arisen!
May sin no more our souls oppress,
And bind in darksome prison.

Let those that lie in slumber fast,
Because the darkness reigns,
The light behold, and straightway cast
Aside their gloomy chains;

And greet the light that makes them free,
The bounding joy it brings;
And share the calm felicity,
That looks to heaven and sings.

O Jesus Christ, our hearts aglow,
Thy blessed advent hail;
On us Thy healing virtue show,
And o'er our ills prevail.

And let us walk as those whose eyes
Have seen the light of heaven,
Till light shall in our souls arise,
Whence night and gloom are driven.

4.

Rise, thou glorious orb of day,
Draw the curtains from the sky;
Let thy light in glad array,
All creation beautify;
Bid the fears of darkness born,
Melt before the light of morn.

Light transcendent! fill the skies,
Glorious Orb of heavenly light!
Take the darkness from our eyes,
Fill our souls with visions bright.
Jesus, Light of lights, appear,
Rise upon our souls with cheer.

From Thy throne of splendour bright,
Shed Thy glory far abroad;
Let the wanderers in their plight
See the path that leads to God,
And upon their pathway shine,
Heavenly Orb of light Divine.

There no sun illumes the day,
Where the wanderers find their rest;
Moon nor stars their light display
In the kingdom of the blest;
For the Christ Himself is Sun,
And the day is never done.

5.

Up, up, my soul! with gladness rise,
And greet the ever-brightening skies.
The morn hath come, sweet morn, awake!
And from thy pinions slumber shake.

Pure as the morn God's presence shines;
Love like its beams, thy life entwines;
Richer the gifts thy God bestows
Than morning beauty can disclose.

Sweet as the breath that fans the bowers,
And stirs the leaves and opening flowers,
Comes with the morn, the breath Divine
To stir thee, slumbering soul of mine.

O Thou, the Morn, the Light, the Sun,
With Thee be every day begun;
Brightness shall clothe my life always,
And fill my soul with grateful praise.

Glory to Thee, O Christ my Lord!
Light of my soul, Incarnate Word!
Come with the morn, abide alway,
And cheer my course to endless day.

6.

The crimson blush of morning glows
On towering peaks where clouds repose;
And, lo! the sombre robe of night
Is rent with shafts of golden light.

O Light Divine, each opening day
Illume our souls with gladdening ray;
And, as the sun his course pursues,
With growing light our lives diffuse.

In childhood's morn, when wondering eyes
Behold the light that fills the skies;
And loins are girt at opening day
Life's myriad voices to obey:

O Light Divine, serene and pure,
Shine on a path of life, secure;
Let joy, like songs the morn that greet,
Make music for the willing feet.

When, prompted by the will of God,
A path we tread, before untrod;
And doubts our onward course attend,
Thy light upon our path extend.

O Light of lights, when day is done,
And night pursues our setting sun,
Be ours to hail that better day,
Whose light Thou art eternally.

7.

The morn awakes; from eastern hills
The golden light creation fills;
And arrows chase the night that flies
Before the ever-brightening skies.

The morn awakes; up, soul of mine!
And, like the morn, in beauty shine;
Strong, as the high-ascending sun,
Thy race of duty boldly run.

Night for the weary comes at length;
Morn gives the soul the needed strength;
Light shall thy path encircling, cheer,
And melt each lingering cloud of fear.

O Light of lights, when night descends,
And brooding fear my life attends,
Show to my soul, that night departs
When morning trims her glowing darts.

O Christ, who art my better Sun,
Bright shines the day with Thee begun;
No terror can the mind oppress,
Nor cloud th' aspiring soul distress.

To Thee, O glorious Light of light,
Be honour paid when morn is bright;
To Father, and to Spirit blest,
Be glory every day exprest.

8.

JAM META NOCTIS TRANSIIT
Hilary of Poitiers, 350

Gone are the shades of night,
The hours of rest are o'er;
New beauties sparkle bright,
And heaven is light once more.

To Thee our prayers shall speed,
O Lord of light Divine;
Come to our utmost need,
And in our darkness shine.

Spirit of love and light,
May we Thine image know,
And in Thy glory bright,
To full perfection grow.

Hear us, O Father blest,
Save us, O Christ the Son;
Thou Comforter the best,
Lead us till life is done.

9.

Lo, in its brightness the morning arising,
Gold on the hilltops in richness is spread;
Heaven decks the earth with a beauty surprising,
Light is the victor, and darkness hath fled.

Lord of the morning, our souls are awaking,
Flood them with beauty, and free them from gloom;
Morn speaks of joy, for when morning was breaking,
Free from death's bands Thou didst rise from the tomb.

Souls that in slumber behold not the beauty,
See not the Master arise in His might;
Hear not the call to the doing of duty,
Know not the rapture that thrills in the light.

Morn speaks of life--let us rise to new living,
Rise with the Lord to the freedom He gives;
Give to the world what the morning is giving,
Hope that was born in the darkness, and lives.

Lo, in its brightness the morning arising:
Lord of the morning, our darkness dispel;
Shine in our souls, till, the sordid despising,
Rise we from earth in Thy presence to dwell.

10.

From the hills the light is streaming,
Hail, the gladsome morn!
Earth with busy life is teeming,
For the day is born.

Dawn, Thou Light of lights, undying,
On a fairer day,
All creation beautifying
With Thy glorious ray.

Weary eyes the hills are scanning
For the early gleam;
Souls, Thy long delay unmanning,
Sleep, and idly dream.

Ah, my soul, be up and doing,
Life will soon be done;
Night, the day is close pursuing
To the setting sun.

And the day of God shall waken
To the soul with fear,
If, the call of life forsaken,
We are slumbering here.

From the hills the light is streaming,
Hail the gladsome morn!
And the light of God is beaming--
This, His day, is born.

11.

ater arches, aperanton
Cento from se ton aphthiton monarchen
By Gregory of Nazianzus, b. 329

O Light that knew no dawn,
That shines to endless day,
All things in earth and heaven
Are lustred by Thy ray;
No eye can to Thy throne ascend,
Nor mind Thy brightness comprehend.

Thy grace, O Father, give,
That I may serve in fear;
Above all boons, I pray,
Grant me Thy voice to hear;
From sin Thy child in mercy free,
And let me dwell in light with Thee.

That, cleansed from filthy stain,
I may meet homage give,
And, pure in heart, behold
And serve Thee while I live;
Clean hands in holy worship raise,
And Thee, O Christ my Saviour, praise.

In supplication meek
To Thee I bend the knee;
O Christ, when Thou shalt come,
In love remember me,
And in Thy kingdom, by Thy grace,
Grant me a humble servant's place.

Thy grace, O Father, give,
I humbly Thee implore;
And let Thy mercy bless
Thy servant more and more.
All grace and glory be to Thee
From age to age eternally.

12.

The morn in beauty breaks,
The world to life awakes:
Up, soul of mine, and sing!
And let the day begun,
In hours of service run,
And joy to duty bring.

The darkness fades away,
Light ushers in the day--
Let there be light for me!
That round my path no cloud
Dark folding may enshroud
Me in perplexity.

To Father and to Son,
To Spirit, Three in One,
Eternal praise be given:
Sung by the saints above,
In songs of fervent love,
Up in the choirs of heaven.

13. Evening
Se kai nun eulogoumen

Now at this evening hour,
O Thou, my Christ, to Thee,
Thou Word of God, Eternal Light,
All grateful praises be.

From Thee the Spirit comes,
Third beam of peerless light,
And in Thyself one glorious orb
The triple rays unite.

Thy word and wisdom Thou
To lighten man hast given,
That he the splendour might reflect
That shines superb in heaven;

And having light within,
Might see Thine image bright,
And daily rise, till he himself
Is altogether light.

14.

Fades the glory of the west--
All the crimson and the gold,
Night allures the world to rest
'Neath her mantle's dusky fold.

Ah, my soul, when night descends,
Fear lest slumber bind thee fast,
And the Bridegroom with His friends,
To the marriage hasten past.

He may come--what soul can know?--
When the sun has gone from sight,
When the stars in myriads glow
In the middle of the night.

Think not thou may'st safely dream
Of His coming by and by,
When the morning's early gleam
Wakes the slumberer, from the sky.

Wake, awake, the time is near,
Trim thy lamp, and tend its light;
For the Bridegroom may appear
In the middle of the night.

15.

See where the orb of day
In glory sinks to rest,
The clouds of gold and purple crown
The mountains of the west;
And eve in silence brings
The night on dusky wings.

It is the hour of peace,
And hearts to heaven ascend:
Come with your burdens and your care,
To an unchanging Friend;
And let the passing day
Bear all your fears away.

It is the hour of prayer;
Let every fault be known;
Unveil the secrets of the soul,
And every sin disown;
The blood for sinners spilt,
Shall bear away your guilt.

It is the hour of praise;
Let joy the stillness break;
And every grateful thought of God
To living song awake;
And saints in heaven shall bear
To God your fervent prayer.

The night in silence falls:
O God, to Thee be praise!
And to the Spirit and the Son,
Throughout the endless days;
Eternal Three in One,
While endless ages run.

16.

There is no darkness where Thou art,
O Jesus Christ, Thou Light serene;
Clouds fold their curtains and depart,
And darkness melts where Thou art seen.

Fair Morning Star! more glorious Sun!
Thou Light of lights, Thy beams display,
Till darkness owns the victory won,
And night is lost in endless day.

Where slumbering souls in bondage lie,
Because the night hath hemmed them in,
Descend, as morning from the sky,
And wake them from their sleep of sin.

Where sorrow dims the downcast eye,
And luring hope is lost to view,
With light the tear-drops beautify,
As sunlight on the morning dew.

O Jesus Christ, Thy light is life;
Shine on our souls and life revive,
That they may stand before the strife,
And conquer as the strong who strive.

O Jesus Christ, Thy light is joy;
Restore our souls from sorrow's blight,
And win them to the glad employ
Of those who praise both day and night.

17.

Lord, upon our night descending,
Bid the light with gladness shine;
Let its rays, through darkness wending,
Round our fears in beauty twine.

Thou art Light, and where Thou dwellest,
Like a traveller, gloom departs;
Come, who threatening clouds dispellest,
And abide within our hearts.

Ah, the visions Thou impartest,
With the morn, and with the noon;
With what glory Thou attirest
Eve, that falleth late or soon.

Flood our lives with varied beauty,
Morn, and noon, and coming night;
Light us in the path of duty,
And at eve let there be light.

18.

Lord, let my evening prayer
As incense sweet ascend;
And while I lift my hands to Thee,
From heaven in mercy bend.

For in Thy name I hope,
And brightness floods my way;
The night departs, and clouds that roll,
And threaten with dismay.

And in Thy name I trust,
To find Thy promise sure;
Thy cov'nant like the mountains strong,
That evermore endure.

Now, at this evening hour,
My hope and trust renew;
Refresh me as the earth that drinks
The cool refreshing dew.

And when the morning wakes,
Awake my soul, I pray,
That in Thy strength goes forth to bear
The burdens of the day.

19.

O Lord of light, Thy beams display,
And waken joy in every heart;
Bring to our souls the light of day,
And bid our brooding night depart.

In Thy fair realm there is no gloom,
The radiant day is never done;
They need no candle to illume,
Nor wait the rising of the sun.

No morning ushers in the day,
Nor evening marks its slow decline;
There Thou art Sun, and shinest aye,
And all the light and joy are Thine.

Eternal Light, Eternal Day,
No eve obscures, no darkness hides;
But clear the noon-tide shines alway,
For there Thy presence aye abides.

Come at this hour, O Light Divine,
As daylight fades, and night is nigh;
And in our souls with radiance shine,
As Thou art wont in realms on high.

20.

kurie eleeson. 'Antilabou, soson, eleeson kai diaphulaxon emas
Litany of the Deacon

God of all grace, Thy mercy send;
Let Thy protecting arm defend;
Save us, and keep us to the end:
Have mercy, Lord.

And through the coming hours of night,
Fill us, we pray, with holy light;
Keep us all sinless in Thy sight:
Grant this, O Lord.

May some bright messenger abide
For ever by Thy servants' side,
A faithful guardian and our guide:
Grant this, O Lord.

From every sin in mercy free,
Let heart and conscience stainless be,
That we may live henceforth for Thee:
Grant this, O Lord.

We would not be by care opprest,
But in Thy love and wisdom rest--
Give what Thou seest to be best:
Grant this, O Lord.

While we of every sin repent,
Let our remaining years be spent
In holiness and sweet content:
Grant this, O Lord.

And when the end of life is near,
May we, unshamed and void of fear,
Wait for the Judgment to appear:
Grant this, O Lord.

21.

The day fades into night,
The shadows lengthening fall,
And see, the deepening purple light
Throws on the hills its pall:
Lord, be our Light when suns decline,
And in our souls unclouded shine.

Still is the eventide,
Calm is the soft repose,
When earthly toil is laid aside,
And eyelids drooping, close;
Lord, let Thy peace my soul possess,
In everlasting restfulness.

Night of my life draws near;
Lord, when the light departs,
Be all to me that Thou hast been
To other trusting hearts,
And in the calm that night bestows,
Let me in peace with Thee repose.

The night gives place to morn,
The gloom shall pass away,
And an eternal day be born,
Whose sun shall shine for aye;
Lord, wake me when the morn is come,
And let me find with Thee my home.

22.

A crown of gold surpassing rare,
The western hills, in beauty wear;
And earth and sea reflect the light,
That fades before th' approach of night.

O Glorious Sun! whose peerless ray
Illumes the realm of endless day,
Shine on a world where darkness dwells,
And all the joy of day dispels.

Soft o'er the land the twilight creeps;
Night falls apace, and nature sleeps;
Oh, let not night my life control,
And plunge in sleep my drowsy soul.

Sleep to the weary pilgrim give,
But let the soul through slumber live;
Wake when the first faint gleam of morn
Tells that another day is born.

Light of my life! bid night depart,
Sing to my soul, and cheer my heart;
That morn, and noon, and night may be
One beauteous day of joy to me.

And when the brightest morn shall break,
And bid the eternal day awake,
O glorious Sun! in radiance shine,
To guard from night the realm Divine.

23.

epseusamen se ten aletheian, loge
Gregory of Nazianzus, b. 329

O Word of Truth! in devious paths
My wayward feet have trod;
I have not kept the day serene
I gave at morn to God.

And now 'tis night, and night within;
O God, the light hath fled!
I have not kept the vow I made
When morn its glories shed.

For clouds of gloom from nether world
Obscured my upward way;
O Christ the Light, Thy light bestow
And turn my night to day!

24. Christmas

Rosy dawn, with locks of gold,
Looks upon the world awaking;
For the day by prophets told,
Lo, in beauty now is breaking,
And the Christ is come to earth:
Hail, all hail His wondrous birth.

Minstrels from the realms of light,
Bend to earth to sing His praises,
For, from depth to highest height,
God our fallen race upraises;
Now the Christ is come to earth,
Hail, all hail His wondrous birth.

Go to Bethlehem, wanderers lone,
Seek the Christ, for whom such glory
Flashing from the heavenly throne
Floods with light the ancient story:
For the Christ is come to earth,
Hail, all hail His wondrous birth.

There, in weakness see Him lie,
Cradled where His mother laid Him,
Who, by minstrels from the sky,
Hath immortal honours paid Him;
See the God-man come to earth,
Hail, all hail His wondrous birth.

King Immortal! treasures rare,
Gifts of heart and life we bring Thee;
Hearts and voices everywhere,
More than gold--their praises bring Thee;
Thou, O Christ, art come to earth,
Hail, all hail Thy wondrous birth.

25.

In the early morning,
Ere the darkness clears,
Lo, a star most radiant,
High in heaven appears;
And their eyes behold it,
Glowing like a gem,
As the sages journey
Forth to Bethlehem.

In the early morning,
While the shepherds gaze,
Lo, through clouds asunder,
Heaven is all ablaze;
Brighter than the sunrise
From the eastern hills,
And the song of angels
All creation fills.

In the early morning,
When the silence hung,
'Mid the dazzling splendour,
Were the praises sung:
Glory in the highest
To the God of heaven,
Peace on earth abounding
Unto men be given.

Now the sages, guided
To the lowly place,
Lying in a manger
Find the Lord of grace;
And they fall before Him
As before a king,
And their costly offerings
With devotion bring.

Lord of life eternal,
Who didst come for men;
At the time appointed
Thou wilt come again;
Not a babe in meekness,
Born of humble birth;
But the King Immortal,

Judge of all the earth.

Glory in the highest,
Be ascribed to God;
Ceaseless hallelujahs
Fill the earth abroad;
Glory to Immanuel,
All creation sing,
Who to heaven hath raised us
By His offering.

26.

Lo, the clouds of night are rending,
Clad in light, heavenly bright,
Herald hosts to earth descending,
Hail approaching morn.

Hail the morn with heavenly singing,
And the song, they prolong,
News untold to earth is bringing,
Of Immanuel born.

Fearful watchers, see the glory,
Cease to gaze with amaze;
Herdsmen, sages, list the story,
Peace abides on earth.

Glory! sons of men repeat it,
Heavenly morn, Christ is born,
Lift your eyes to heaven and greet it,
Greet Immanuel's birth.

Gone the dismal years of waiting,
Angels bright, shed your light!
Peace hath banished ill and hating,
On this glorious morn.

Glory be to God ascending,
And the Son, who hath won
Life for man in bliss unending,
Now the Christ is born.

27.

Herdsmen keeping lonely vigil
While the earth in slumber lay;
Eager scanned the far horizon,
For the coming of the day;
And a blaze of heavenly light,
Rent the curtains of the night.

Never shone a morn so radiant
Since creation had its birth,
And the orb of day in fulness
Shed its primal light on earth,
And the morning stars abroad,
Triumphed with the sons of God.

Stay your coming, dawn and sunrise,
For a Sun of high renown
Pours His light upon our darkness,
And this Orb shall ne'er go down;
Now Immanuel, Christ our Lord,
Dwells on earth, Incarnate Word.

Lift your eyes, ye lonely watchers,
See the host in raiment white;
List, the strains of heavenly music
Mingling with transcendent light;
Ne'er such music waked a morn;
Sons of men! the Christ is born.

Weary hearts that dwell in darkness!
Cast your dismal fears away;
Lo, the Sun on earth is shining,
For the morn has risen today,
And the light that hailed His birth,
Pours its glory on the earth.

28.

oi magoi ta d?ra prospherousin
oi poimenes to thauma keruttousin

Hail to the King, who comes in weakness now,
No wreath of gold encircleth His brow,
Lowly His state--in lowly worship bow;
Hail to the King!

Born of His maiden mother, pure as snow,
Son of our God, begotten long ago,
Ere yet the stream of time began to flow;
Hail to the King!

Nowhere was found a shelter for His head,
Humble He lay, e'en where the oxen fed,
No couch nor crib, a manger was His bed;
Hail to the King!

Herdsmen were there who heard the angels sing;
Wise men from far who myrrh and incense bring,
No other hand bestowed an offering;
Hail to the King!

Hail to the King! O Christ, upon Thy throne,
Look on the souls which Thou didst make Thine own,
When by Thy birth and death Thou didst atone;
Hail to the King!

29.

Doxa en upsistois The?

Hark! upon the morning breezes,
In the darkness, ere the waking,
Music sweet the senses pleases,
Soft upon the stillness breaking;
"Glory, Glory!" this the singing,
Welcome to Immanuel bringing.

Shepherds at their watch beholding
Angels clad in glistening whiteness,
Heard the wondrous news unfolding
'Mid that dazzling scene of brightness:
"Glory, Glory!" peace, and kindness,
Light is breaking on our blindness.

Glorious morn! The sun, uprising,
Shone upon a world rejoicing;
God is with us--truth surprising!
List to song the message voicing:
"Glory, Glory!" ages told it,
Heavenly voices now unfold it.

God adored, our nature wearing!
Ah, such condescending meekness!
Stooping to a world despairing,
Full of pity for our weakness:
"Glory, Glory!" praises swelling,
God hath made with man His dwelling.

30.

techthentos tou Christou

Hail to the morn that dawns on eastern hills,
More radiant far than any earthly morn;
'Tis heavenly light that all creation fills--
The Christ is born.

Mystery profound, through all the ages sealed,
Now, to a world all hopeless, and forlorn,
In Bethlehem's manger is at length revealed--
The Christ is born.

Lo, from their watch the herdsmen raise their eyes,
For, dazzling light the robe of night had torn,
And angels poured their raptures from the skies--
The Christ is born.

Bring ye your gifts of gold and incense rare,
Wise men who come, all travel-stained and worn;
Find ye the Child, and pay your homage there--
The Christ is born.

Hail to the morn, the world exulting sings;
Only to Him, in fealty we are sworn,
Lord of our lives, Immortal King of kings!--
The Christ is born.

31.

Deute agalliasometha t? churio, to paron musterion ekdiegoumenoi

Come, let us sing with joyful mirth
The mystery of Immanuel's birth,
Who, virgin born, is here;
The middle wall no longer stands,
No flaming sword in cherub's hands
Inspires the soul with fear.

See, clear the pathway open lies
That upward leads to Paradise,
Where stands the Tree of Life;
And freely may I enter in,
Whence I was driven by mortal sin,
And worsted in the strife.

For He, the Father's only Son,
A glorious work hath now begun,
Descending from above
In servant's form, though yet the Son,
Unchanging while the ages run,
To win us by His love.

Come, now, let hearts united be
To laud His praises joyfully,
The God-Man born to-day.
And let Thy mercy reach us now,
For pitiful and kind art Thou,
O Virgin born, we pray.

32.

PUER NATUS IN BETHLEHEM
From a Latin MS. of the Early 14th Century

Zion is glad this glorious morn:
A Babe in Bethlehem is born.

See where He lies in manger low,
Whose kingly reign no end shall know.

The ox and ass that filled the stall,
Knew that the Babe was Lord of all.

Out from the east the sages bring
Their treasures for an offering.

They humbly seek the lowly place,
And worship there the King of grace:

The Son of God, who made the earth,
A virgin mother gave Him birth.

No poison from the serpent stains
The human blood that fills His veins;

And though our flesh He meekly wears,
No mark of sin His nature bears;

That He might man to God restore,
And give the grace that once He wore.

Come, while our hearts are full of mirth,
And bless the Lord of lowly birth.

The Holy Trinity we'll praise,
And give our thanks to God always.

33.

Out from the rising of the sun,
O'er tracts of desert wild,
The Magi came on journey lone,
To seek the heaven-born Child;
The star o'erhead their footsteps led,
And hope their way beguiled.

They bore Him costly gifts of gold,
And myrrh and spices sweet:
"For He is King," they had been told,
Whom they would meekly greet;
And they would go, in reverence low,
And worship at His feet.

O humble Child, in manger laid!
The wise beheld Thee there,
And reverently their homage paid,
And gave their offerings rare.
Their quest was found, and to the ground
They bowed the head in prayer.

O Jesu, who in manger lay,
The Son of God most high,
Let me my humble homage pay,
And bring my offerings nigh.
And humbly greet Thee at Thy feet,
And low in worship lie.

34.

ti soi prosenenkomen, Christe
By St. Anatolius, 458 A.D.

What shall we bring to Thee?
What shall our offering be
On this Thy natal morn?
For Thou, O Christ, hast come to earth--
A virgin mother gave Thee birth--
For our redemption born.

The whole creation broad
Gives praise and thanks to God,
Who gave His only Son;
And list! the bright angelic throng
Their homage yield in sweetest song,
For peace on earth begun.

The heavens their glory shed,
The star shines o'er His head,
The promised Christ and King;
And wise men from the lands afar,
Led by the brightness of the star,
Their treasured offerings bring.

What shall we give Thee now?
Lowly the shepherds bow,
Have we no gift to bring?
Our worship, lo, we yield to Thee,
All that we are, and hope to be--
This is our offering.

35.

Over trackless regions,
From the Morning land,
Bearing costly treasures,
Came a seeking band--
Wise men with devotion,
From the Morning land.

Wheresoe'er the star led,
In the ebon sky,
Thither pressed those wise men,
With uplifted eye,
Following the star light
In the ebon sky.

They would find the young King
Whom the star foretold;
They would render homage,
And their gifts unfold,
Bowing low before Him,
Whom the star foretold.

Jesu, Son of David,
God's Incarnate Word,
Endless, unbegotten,
By the wise adored--
We would bow before Thee,
God's Incarnate Word.

Not without an offering
Would we seek our King;
But with true devotion
What is noblest, bring--
With a gift so precious,
Would we seek our King.

Jesu, King Eternal,
Son of God, Divine,
Man, yet still remaining
Of the Godbead Trine--
See, our hearts we give Thee,
Son of God, Divine.

36.

Doxa en upsistois The?
By St. John of Damascus, 780 A.D.

Bethlehem rejoices!
Hark the voices clear,
Singing in the starlight
Nearer and more near.
Unto God be glory,
Peace to men be given;
This His will who dwelleth
In the heights of heaven.

Heaven cannot contain Him,
Nor the bounds of earth,
Yet, oh glorious mystery!
Virgin gives Him birth.
Unto God be glory,
Peace to men be given;
This His will who dwelleth
In the heights of heaven.

Now the light ariseth
In the darkened skies,
Now the proud are humbled
And the lowly rise.
Unto God be glory,
Peace to men be given;
This His will who dwelleth
In the heights of heaven.

37.

angeloi meta poimenon doxazousi

A band of herdsmen tarried late,
Through hours of night disconsolate;
Around, the snow lay glistening white,
And stars o'erhead were shining bright;
O favoured shepherds, there shall rise
A brighter star in yonder skies.

Whence comes this glory, brighter far
Than light that shines from midnight star?
An angel from the Lord appears,
And lo! their minds are filled with fears;
O favoured shepherds, wherefore fear?
The messenger of God is here.

"O band of herdsmen, list! I bring
Glad tidings of a promised King;
Go, in a manger ye shall find
The new-born Saviour of mankind";
O favoured shepherds, such surprise!
To see the Christ in mean disguise.

Then stood the herdsmen all amaze,
For heaven with glory was ablaze;
And choirs of angels, clad in white,
Awoke with song the silent night:
O favoured shepherds, ye are blest,
To hear that heavenly song exprest.

"To God be glory," thus they sang,
While earth and heaven with music rang;
"And peace abounding henceforth dwell
With those on earth who please Me well";
O favoured shepherds, night is past,
And morn, bright morn, is come at last.

O band of herdsmen, long ago,
That song was sung on earth below;
Now myriad hosts uplift the strains
That first awoke on Bethlehem's plains:
O favoured shepherds, round the throne,
The angel's song is now your own.

38.

Glory in the highest!
Hark, what angels sing:
Was there e'er such music
Borne on rising wing?
See, the gates of heaven
On their portals rise,
And the song that charms us
Comes from Paradise.

Glory in the highest!
Christ our Lord is born;
Hail His glorious advent
On this happy morn;
Ages long have waited
'Mid their brooding ills;
Now the herald-voices
Wake the silent hills.

Herdsmen in their watching
Lift their eyes amazed;
Sages from the sunland
At the starlight gazed;
And they bear their treasures,
Gold for diadem,
Meet to crown the Monarch
Born at Bethlehem.

Glory in the highest!
With the sages bring
What is best and fairest
For an offering;
Lay before the manger
Where the Infant lies,
All your heart's devotion,
Love's best sacrifice.

39.

Christos gennatai
By St. Cosmas the Melodist, 760 A.D.

Christ is born, go forth to meet Him,
Christ by all the heaven adored;
Singing songs of welcome, greet Him,
For the earth receives her Lord.
All ye nations, shout and sing;
For He comes, your glorious King.

Once His heavenly image bearing,
Man has sunk to depths of sin;
Now defiled, debased, despairing,
Clad in rags and foul within;
But our God, who beauty gave,
Lifts the soul He comes to save.

From the height of heaven beholding,
Pity filled the heart of grace;
And our Lord, His love unfolding,
Made the earth His dwelling-place;
And a virgin mother gave
God Incarnate, man to save.

Wisdom, Might, and Word Eternal,
Glory of the Father, Thou!
Hid from man and powers supernal,
Lo, He wears our nature now!
To the Lord your worship bring,
Praise Him, your victorious King.

40. Palm Sunday

Behold the Lord to Zion rides,
And crowds hosannas sing;
They spread their garments in the way,
And hail Him as a king.

O Zion, blind with earthly pride,
Why couldst thou not behold
The Christ of God, whom sage and seer
From age to age foretold?

A King indeed, but not to reign
By power of earthly might;
The glory of whose royal state
Is hid from carnal sight.

Whose subjects are the souls of men
From thrall of darkness won;
Whose kingdom knows no bounds, within
The dawn and setting sun.

Behold thy King to Zion rides
Where He the cross shall bear;
And on that throne with blood bedecked,
His robe of purple wear;

Where slaves to sin His love shall view,
And from their bondage rise
To noble fealty, by the power
Of loving sacrifice.

41.

O God of love, whose mercy came
To this dark world of sin and shame,
And on a cross of suffering sore,
That sin and shame in meekness bore.

Supreme the love the Christ displayed,
When He, True God, True Man was made;
When He was scorned, His patience then
Shone forth Divine, with sinful men.

Did e'er such mercy lead the great
To stoop from high to low estate?
Did e'er such love incline the heart
To take the erring sinner's part?

'Twas God who loved, 'twas God who gave
His Son our erring souls to save;
'Tis Christ that wins us by the love
From earth below to heaven above.

Win me, O Lord, whose mercy came
To this dark world of sin and shame,
To that bright world whose beauties shine
For ever in Thy love Divine.

To Thee, O Father, glory be;
And glory, Christ, God-Man, to Thee;
And to the Spirit, Three in One,
Now, and while countless ages run.

42.

Christos o Logos me theoi sarkoumenos

Christ the Word! Thine incarnation
Links my nature to Thine own;
By Thy sore humiliation,
I am lifted to Thy throne;
By Thy suffering Thou hast fired me
With a zeal to sacrifice,
And to noble life inspired me:
Hence my grateful songs arise.

Word of God! Thy crucifixion
Hath upraised me from the earth;
By Thy death and dereliction,
Thou hast given me nobler birth;
By Thy resurrection glorious,
Life immortal now I own:
Hence ascend my songs victorious
To Thy praise, O Christ the Son.

By Thy hand at the creation,
Thou didst form me from the ground,
And, to mark my kingly station,
With Thine image I was crowned;
And that hand, when pierced and bleeding,
Raised me from corruption's mire;
And, though all this love unheeding,
Decked me with Divine attire.

Thou who gav'st my soul its being,
Breathing in me life Divine,
Didst, by Thine all-wise decreeing,
Unto death Thy life resign;
And from death my soul defending,
Thou didst sojourn with the dead,
That Thou might'st, my fetters rending,
Raise me up, Thou glorious Head!

Shame be on your heads abiding,
Disobedient people now,
Who to death, and vile deriding,

Caused the Word of God to bow!
Shame! for death, nor powers infernal,
Nor the dark of hades' gloom,
Could retain the King Eternal
In the bondage of the tomb.

43. Easter

Glory to God! The morn appointed breaks,
And earth awakes from all the woeful past;
For, with the morn, the Lord of Life awakes,
And sin and death into the grave are cast.

Glory to God! The cross, with all its shame,
Now sheds its glory o'er a ransomed world;
For He who bore the burden of our blame,
With pierced hands the foe to hell hath hurled.

Glory to God! Sing ransomed souls again,
And let your songs our glorious Victor laud,
Who by His might hath snapped the tyrant's chain,
And set us free to rise with Him to God.

Darkness and night, farewell! the morn is here;
Welcome! the light that ushers in the day;
Visions of joy before our sight appear,
And like the clouds, our sorrows melt away.

Great Son of God, Immortal and renowned!
Brighter than morn the glory on Thy brow;
Crowns must be won, and Thou art nobly crowned,
For death is dead, and sin is vanquished now.

44.

tas esperinas em?n euchas

Accept our evening prayer,
O Holy Christ our Lord,
And grant forgiveness of our sin
According to Thy word,
Who, by Thy rising, hast revealed
A power that lay from man concealed.

Oh come, ye people, come,
Give praise to Christ your God;
The glory of His rising tell
To all the world abroad:
For He is God, whose power hath hurled
The great accuser from the world.

Encompass Zion round,
And in her midst proclaim
The glory of the Son of God,
Who back from bondage came;
Who burst the gates of death, to win
Our freedom from the yoke of sin.

Thy Passion, Lord, hath freed
Our souls from passion's reign;
Nor may we know corruption base,
Since Thou hast risen again;
Glory to Thee, O Christ the Lord,
Son of our God, Incarnate Word!

45.

anastasin Christou theasamenoi

We have heard the wondrous story
Of the Resurrection morn;
We have seen its matchless glory,
Christ the risen Lord adorn.
Let us worship and adore Him,
Let us now fall down before Him.

Men with erring sinners found Thee,
Found the only sinless One;
And upon a cross they bound Thee,
For the good that Thou hadst done;
Let us worship and adore Him,
Let us now fall down before Him.

We have heard the wondrous story
Of the Resurrection morn:
Christ our God, to Him be glory,
For the bands of death are torn;
Let us worship and adore Him,
Come and let us fall before Him.

Come, ye faithful, come with gladness,
To your God thanksgiving pay;
For the Cross was shorn of sadness
On the Resurrection day:
Let us worship and adore Him,
Come and let us bow before Him.

46.

He led them forth to Bethany,
And with uplifted hand,
Invoked abiding blessing there,
Upon His chosen band.

And while He climbed the heavenly path,
His followers with amaze
Beheld the Christ from earth ascend,
Beyond their farthest gaze.

O Christ, our Lord, ascended now,
The Kingdom is Thine own;
And angel hosts in triumph lead
The Victor to His throne.

But think upon the days of woe,
The sorrow and the pain,
And visit with Thy gracious help
Thy followers again.

That they may stand while others fall,
And fight while others flee,
And on the cross their arms extend
In loyalty to Thee.

And raise them to the calm of heaven
When all the strife is past,
Where saints behold Thee and adore
While endless ages last.

47.

See the King of kings ascending
To His throne of power again;
Who in humble garb descending,
Came to dwell with lowly men.

Glad the angel hosts adoring
Fling the golden gates aside;
Mortals, view the Victor soaring,
Heaven receives the Lord with pride.

Strike your harps, ye choirs supernal;
Lift your songs of welcome now;
For behold, your King eternal
Comes with laurels on His brow.

Gone the sorrow and the sighing,
All the anguish and the pain;
Gone the weakness and the dying--
Choirs immortal, raise the strain:

Hallelujah! endless glory
To the King of Glory give;
Mortals, heed the gladsome story,
Christ is risen, and thou may'st live!

48.

kai ten pros upsos ouranou theian anlepsin

He mounts to where the azure shines,
Triumphant as the light;
Till, past the glowing gates, the Christ
Is lost to mortal sight.

And now, amid the bliss of heaven,
The Father's throne He shares;
And gems of radiant beauty deck
The sparkling crown He wears.

Remember, Lord, Thy promise made
When hearts in sadness pined,
And send the Comforter to soothe
The sorrows of mankind;

And as the lingering ages pass,
To teach the souls of men
That they may hail the Christ when He
In glory comes again.

All praise to Thee, Eternal God,
And to the Son be given,
Whose glory, darkly veiled on earth,
Now fills the light of heaven;

And to the Holy Comforter,
By whom our lives are blest,
Be praise, by every waiting heart,
For evermore expressed.

49.

Past the cross with all its shame,
All its grief and gloom;
Past the solitude of death
In the silent tomb:
Lo, the Victor from the strife,
Giver of Immortal life.

Stands He there on Olivet,
With an outstretched hand,
Calling His last blessing down,
On His faithful band,
Ere He mounts the azure height
Past the range of mortal sight.

Bow, ye heavens, in reverence low;
Clouds, a pathway clear;
For the Christ, who came to earth,
Mounts the glowing sphere;
Stand, ye heavenly gates, aside,
For He enters to abide.

Angels look with wondering gaze,
As their Lord draws nigher;
Why these wounded hands and feet?
And that stained attire?
Hail! the God-man from the strife,
Wins for man immortal life.

All alone, the faithful gaze
Towards the silent skies;
For the Christ hath passed beyond
Love's enquiring eyes;
But our flesh is knit to His
Where the ascended God-man is.

50. Pentecost

Oh, may the Spirit of all grace
Descend and in our hearts abide,
And what of good or ill betide,
Find in them aye a resting-place.

There is no peace to mortals given,
Save when the Spirit finds His rest
Within the secret of our breast,
And there inspires the calm of heaven.

Our earthly calms a storm presage;
They whisper peace, and tempests rise;
And clouds obscure the brightest skies,
And winds and waves in tumult rage.

No storm disturbs the heavenly peace;
No whispering fills the soul with fears
As when the brooding tempest nears,
And clouds around our path increase.

'Tis lasting calm, 'tis heavenly rest:
Come, Spirit of the Living God,
And in our spirits shed abroad
The peace that makes the troubled blest.

51.

To God the Holy Ghost
Let homage due be paid,
Who, when we sorrow most,
Comes with His heavenly aid,
And speaks the word alluring, kind,
That fills with peace the anxious mind.

Then winds their raging cease,
And billows sink to rest;
Our souls repose in peace,
As child on mother's breast;
Blest Spirit! there is naught to fear,
When Thou, our Comforter, art near.

Come then, Thou gracious Guest,
Our earnest prayers ascend;
Prepare Thyself a rest,
Abide our constant Friend;
Fulfil the promise Jesus made,
When sorrow on His soul was laid.

Oh, bid our darkness flee,
And with Thy light come in;
Our souls from trouble free,
And from the thrall of sin:
Blest Spirit! condescending, come,
And make our souls Thy chosen home.

52.

Spirit of Light, Thy glory pour,
And let mine eyes Thy radiance see;
From sin's dark night my soul restore,
To dwell in light for aye with Thee.

Spirit of Love, whose heavenly wiles
Can lure the heart from meaner bonds,
Come to my life as love that smiles,
And wakens love that quick responds.

Spirit of Grace, with gifts more rare
Than all the stores of earth possess,
Now to my soul Thy riches bear,
Of pity, love, and tenderness.

Spirit of Light, and Love, and Grace,
Welcome, Thy entrance to my heart;
Take to Thyself its chiefest place,
Who of the triune Godhead art.

53.
basileu ouranie, paraklete

O King enthroned on high,
Thou Comforter Divine,
Blest Spirit of all Truth, be nigh
And make us Thine.

Yea, Thou art everywhere,
All places far or near;
Oh, listen to our humble prayer,
Be with us here!

Thou art the source of life,
Thou art our treasure-store;
Give us Thy peace, and end our strife
For evermore.

Descend, O Heavenly Dove,
Abide with us alway;
And in the fulness of Thy love
Cleanse us, we pray.

54.

Spirit of God, in love descend,
And make our hearts Thy place of rest;
In all our need a steadfast Friend,
To fill our store with gifts the best;

To cleanse our souls with holy fire
From sordid stains that guilt imparts,
And with Thy heavenly power inspire
Our languid zeal, and fainting hearts;

To lift our minds to nobler things
Than earth from all its best can show--
The wealth that flies on speedy wings,
The fleeting joys, like sparks that glow.

Come in the hour of sore distress,
When deep the heart for comfort sighs;
And with Thy soothing kindliness
The tear-drops wipe from weeping eyes.

"Lo, I am with you to the end,"
Thus speaks the promise of our Lord;
O Spirit of the Christ, descend,
Fulfil to us the gracious word.

55.

Lord, may Thy Holy Spirit calm
Our troubled souls, and give them rest;
And with His touch, like healing balm,
Allay the pain of the distressed.

We hear the promise Thou didst make
To lone disciples long ago;
And peace and hope our souls o'ertake,
And joy dispels our brooding woe.

Now let us feel the Spirit's power,
And let us hear His gracious word;
Fulfil to us this holy hour,
The promise of our dying Lord.

Come, Holy Ghost, with warmth of love,
With light of hope, and calm of peace,
And raise our sense-bound souls above
The mocking joys of earth that cease.

56.

'Ergo, os palai mathetais epengeilo

As Thou didst say--the Spirit came
In fiery tongues of living flame;
And men were moved to spread abroad
The wisdom of th' Incarnate God.

And nations heard the truth, and gave
Their souls to Him who came to save;
And toiling in their sins, arose
The power of Satan to oppose.

As Thou didst say--the Spirit's power
Came at the Pentecostal hour;
And drooping souls with zeal were fired,
And felt the life that power inspired.

As Thou didst say--the Spirit's voice
Spake to dull hearts, and bade rejoice;
And men that dwelt in sorrow's night,
Felt hope awake as morning light.

As Thou didst say--His power can still
Our empty lives to fulness fill;
Can charge with hope, with zeal inspire,
And kindle life, and light, and fire.

As Thou didst say--O Spirit, come,
Make with Thy people here Thy home;
In all their need Thy gifts supply,
And Christ our Lord still glorify.

57. Anointing of the sick

O Gracious Christ, Thy power reveal,
And let Thy sin-sick servant live;
Speak but the word, for Thou canst heal,
And from its wounds my soul relieve.

My stricken soul for succour cries,
For Thou, O Lord, compassion art;
Now, while I lift my pleading eyes,
Thy healing grace in love impart.

Thou, Lord, didst journey long ago,
Where sick and sorrowing lives were spent;
And Thou didst heed the call of woe,
And joy and health from heaven were sent.

And Thou hast power to-day as then,
And Thou with love art loving still;
Still art Thou with the sons of men
Thy healing mission to fulfil.

Teach me, O Christ, my rest to find
From all my sickness and my care,
Upon Thy love exceeding kind,
That finds the needy everywhere.

58. Anointing of the sick
tachus eis antilepsin, nomos uparchon Christi

Thou, Lord, hast power to heal,
And Thou wilt quickly aid;
For Thou dost deeply feel
The stripes upon us laid--
Thou who wast wounded by the rod
Uplifted in the hand of God.

Send speedy help, we pray,
To him who ailing lies,
That from his couch he may
With thankful heart arise;
Through prayers which all availing find
Thine ear, O Lover of mankind.

Oh, blinded are our eyes,
And all are held in night;
But like the blind who cries,
We cry to Thee for light;
In penitence, O Christ, we pray,
Give us the radiant light of day.

59. Anointing of the sick
eleous pege, uparchon 'peragathe

A Fount of mercy, Lord, Thou art,
Perennial and Divine;
Thou Source of every lasting good,
All needed grace is Thine;
Now to the sufferer healing give,
And touch the sick, that he may live.

O Saviour, Who alone art God,
Thy hand is quick to heal,
For Thou didst wear our feeble flesh,
And all its ailments feel;
And Thou canst make the sufferer whole,
And save the sin-afflicted soul.

O Christ, the great Physician Thou,
Tender and full of power;
Now with the oil of grace anoint
The sufferer at this hour;
Bid Thou the pain and weakness cease,
And give the sore afflicted peace.

60. Burial Service

ton piston oiketen sou, anapouson os eusplanchnos

Rest in the Lord, O servant by His grace;
Dwell in His courts, and gaze upon His face;
Know naught of toil, of weariness, or woe:
They rest who serve, not weary, as below.

Rest in the Lord: the strife of war is past,
Wear now the wreath of victory at last;
E'en death is slain--the cross of Christ sufficed,
Death is not death, to those who live in Christ.

Rest in the Lord: the goal of life is won,
To thee 'tis given to hear the glad "Well done";
Great their reward who, till their Lord appear,
Serve in the vineyard of the Master, here.

Rest in the Lord: none can His honour claim,
They honour have, who honour most His name;
Thine this reward, who counted gain but loss,
Nor felt it shame to glory in the cross.

Rest in the Lord: swift comes the happy time
When we who strive shall reach Thy fairer clime;
Christ, give us welcome when the toil is past,
And bring us to the bliss of heaven at last.

61.

Almighty God, great Source of all,
Upholder of the earth and sea,
To whom Thy works unceasing call,
Throughout their vast immensity;
The heaven reflects Thy glory bright,
From sunlit dome, and starry height.

Dark clouds surround Thy kingly seat;
But where Thou art is peerless light;
There righteousness and mercy meet
In all their gentleness and might;
The beauty of Thy place of bliss
Is purity and holiness.

Almighty God! Thy power supreme
The rebel arm presumes to win,
While all the hosts of hell blaspheme,
And hurl the darts of death and sin;
But lo, the God-man, girt with might,
Hath turned the hosts of hell to flight.

Almighty God! we lift our eyes
To where the awful cross is raised,
And there, by holy sacrifice,
Behold the pride of sin abased;
And at His feet, whose love o'ercame,
Renew our fealty to Thy name.

62.

Great love Divine, whose compass broad
Involves the utmost point from God;
Wide as the sun its radiance sheds,
Broad as the night its darkness spreads;
Far as the heavens creation span
Reaches the love of God for man.

Great love Divine, far reaching, vast,
To endless time from ages past;
As far as stretches human need,
Far as the sin of man can lead;
No wandering soul outstrips its pace,
Or gains the limit of its grace.

Great love Divine, profoundly deep,
More mysteries than the waters keep
Are held within its vast abyss,
Unsounded, dark, and fathomless;
It sinks to where the hopeless lie,
To touch their deepest misery.

Great love Divine, surpassing far
In height yon glorious morning star;
Brighter its sheen, more pure and fair,
No stain of faithlessness is there;
It beckons from the heavenly throne
Whence from eternity it shone.

Profoundest thought the mind can hold,
Conned by the saints through ages old,
Taught by the Christ whose mission showed
Its greatness by the gift bestowed;
Great love Divine!--immortal theme!
In breadth, length, depth, and height supreme.

63.

Great Son of God, supremely brave,
Who stooped to earth in fleshly guise,
The erring souls of men to save,
And bring them back to Paradise;
Unceasing praise Thy love shall tell,
Where men redeemed, and angels dwell.

Great Son of God, supremely meek,
The vileness of our shame to wear;
In haunts of sin the lost to seek,
The burden of their guilt to bear,
And on a cross resign Thy breath,
To save their souls from endless death.

Great Son of God, supremely good,
The blessing of Thy life to give;
Thy wounded flesh for needful food,
That in Thy strength our souls may live,
And in that strength unfaltering rise
To lives of noblest sacrifice.

Great Son of God, we own Thy claim--
Our souls are Thine, and not our own;
Now on our foreheads stamp Thy name,
That we may live for Thee alone,
And in our lives such service show,
As Thou didst render here below.

64. Preparation for Worship

How shall we climb the hill of God,
And stand before His face--
We, who in heedless ways have trod,
And scorned the thought of grace?

Our hands with guilty deeds are stained,
All that we touch is vile;
The things we sought for, and have gained,
With filthiness defile.

And in our hearts, the home of love,
No love of God resides;
No thought that wings its flight above,
Where purity abides.

But Thou wilt cleanse our filthiness,
And with Thy Spirit's fire
Consume the hateful sordidness,
That taints our souls' desire.

Then shall we climb the holy hill
With those whose hands are clean;
Such visions bright our minds shall fill
As by the pure are seen.

O God, our God, we worship low,
For Thou hast brought us nigh;
Grant us in holiness to grow,
Till we abide on high.

65.

Almighty God! Thy power controls
The surging sea that ceaseless rolls;
Its waves obey Thy high behest,
And mount to heaven, or sink to rest.

Creation owns its rightful Lord,
And bows submissive to Thy word;
No will against Thy will prevails,
He sinks to earth who God assails.

When passions surge within the soul,
As waves before the tempest roll;
When wild desires the heart entice
From yielding aught to sacrifice,

Then, Lord, command the surge to cease,
And give the soul Thy lasting peace;
For Thou hast power who stilled the sea
That wildly raged at Galilee.

Lord, when our souls by care oppressed,
By sorrow grieved, or doubt distressed,
Peer through the darkness for the ray
That tells of dawn, and coming day:

Speak, and the Voice that bade the light
O'erthrow the reign of primal night,
Shall bring the sunshine that shall scare
Those prowling terrors in their lair.

O Christ our Lord, Thy power proclaim,
Our wills control, our passions tame;
Be near us, and unrest shall cease,
Amid the calm of heavenly peace.

66. Penitence

tes patroas doxes sou

Far from Thy heavenly care,
Lord, I have gone astray;
And all the wealth Thou gav'st to me,
Have cast away.

Now from a broken heart,
In penitence sincere,
I lift my prayer to Thee, O Lord;
In mercy hear;

And in Thy blest abode
Give me a servant's place,
That I, a son, may learn to own
A Father's grace.

67.

phos ilaron agais doxes
By Athenogenes, d. 200

Light serene of holy glory
From the Immortal Father poured,
Holy Thou, O blessed Jesus,
Holy, blessed, Christ the Lord.

Now we see the sun descending,
Now declines the evening light,
And in hymns we praise the Father,
Son and Spirit, God of Might.

Worthy of unending praises,
Christ the Son of God, art Thou;
For Thy gift of life eternal,
See the world adores Thee now.

68.

otan elthes o theos epi ges

When Thou shalt come, O Lord,
Wrapt in Thy glory bright,
Then shall the earth in terror quake,
The sun withhold his light.

When Thou shalt come, O Lord,
Then to Thy judgment-bar,
Even as a mighty stream, shall flow
The sons of men from far.

When Thou shalt come, O Lord,
Then save me by Thy power;
Let not the flames of wrath o'ertake
Thy servant in that hour.

When Thou shalt come, O Lord,
In mercy let me stand--
No guilt upon my conscience laid--
Approved, at Thy right hand.

69.

ten achranton eikona sou proskunoumen

To Thy blest Cross, O Christ, we come,
And falling down adore Thee,
And humbly make confession full
Of all our sins before Thee.

For Thou Thyself art very God,
And freely cam'st to save us;
And in our flesh the fetters broke
With which our sins enslave us.

Therefore we own with grateful hearts
The joy the Saviour brought us,
Who came to earth, and in our sins
With love and pity sought us.

70. Consecration

Lord, I am Thine, for Thou hast died for me;
Thy claim I own, and give myself to Thee;
Not with the price of gold, of gold most fine
Hast Thou redeemed my soul, and made me Thine:

Thy blood was shed upon the awful tree;
I marvel at the love there shown for me
All loveless, and to sin and self a slave;
Thy gifts enriched me, yet I nothing gave!

Now in its wonder would my soul arise,
Shorn of all pride, but precious in Thine eyes,
Who for its life Thy glory laidst aside,
And wore its shame, and for its purchase died;

And fired with love, that wondrous love proclaim
In life, in death, in fealty to Thy name;
In loving service, for such service given,
Here upon earth, and yonder in Thy heaven.

Lord, I am Thine, Thy love hath won my soul;
Now shall my life obey such sweet control--
No, not mine own, the purchase is complete,

71. The Burden Bearer

o Soter emon, anatole anatol?n

Come, with the load of sorrow thou art bearing,
Lay it on Him who every burden bears;
Let not thy soul in trouble sink despairing,
He who hath sorrowed, every sorrow shares.

Look for the morn when night is dark and weary,
Morning shall come when hours of night are spent;
Clouds hide the sun, and make the noontide dreary,
Gladness shall cheer you when the clouds are rent.

Look for His smile who gilds the hills at morning;
Surely it comes as comes the morning sun;
Beauty shall grace thy life with bright adorning,
Even as the sunlight, till thy day is done.

Then, when the morn, that makes the hilltops golden
Round the Jerusalem thy spirit gains,
Breaks on thy view, shall come the gladness olden,
Shared by the dwellers in those blest domains.

72.

JESU, LUX HOMINUM

When the morn with golden ray,
Ushers in the new-born day,
Brighter be Thy beams, I pray,
Jesu, Light of men.

When the joys of earth are blest,
When I deem its gifts the best,
Lead me to the land of rest,
Jesu, Light of men.

When the clouds around my head
Fill the soul with doubt and dread,
Let Thy gracious light be shed,
Jesu, Light of men.

When the darkness veils the light,
When the day is lost in night,
Shine in beams of radiance bright,
Jesu, Light of men.

When in night of grief I mourn,
When with pain my heart is torn,
Come in brightness, like the morn,
Jesu, Light of men.

When the vale of death I tread,
Clouds of darkness round my head,
On the path Thy brightness shed,
Jesu, Light of men.

When I dwell in light Divine,
When the bliss of heaven is mine,
Light of lights, all praise be Thine,
Jesu, Light of men.

73.

os egerthe o kurios, thanatosas ton thanaton

Glorious from the field of strife,
Lo! the Victor mounts His throne;
Lord of death and King of life,
His the triumph, His alone--
Glorious from the field of strife,
Christ, Immortal King of Life.

Wake to gladness, sons of men!
Heaven, your gates eternal raise!
Welcome to your bliss again
Him, the worthiest of praise--
Glorious from the field of strife,
Christ, Immortal King of Life.

Ah, the rage of angry foes!
Ah, the garments rolled in blood!
Where were dealt the fiercest blows,
There the valiant Victor stood--
Glorious on the field of strife,
Christ, Immortal King of Life.

Sin and death--the twain assailed,
And the Christ expiring fell;
But the Death o'er death prevailed,
And the might of sin and hell;
Victor from the field of strife,
Hail! Immortal King of Life.

74.

Darkly the tempest swept
Over the sea;
Fiercely the billows leapt,
Bounding and free;
Sternly each rower bent,
While in the firmament
Clouds were by lightnings rent,
O'er Galilee.

Pillowed, the Master lay,
Rocked by the deep;
Worn with the toil of day,
Weary, asleep;
"Master," they fearful cry,
"Wake to the danger nigh;
Winds from the threatening sky,
Billows that leap."

Calmly the Master rose--
Winds are assuaged;
Sank into calm repose
Waters that raged,
"Peace!" O Thou Lord of might,
Speak in our dread affright,
When through our troubled night,
Battles are waged.

75.

JERUSALEM LUMINOSA VERAE PACIS VISIO

O city girt with glory!
Thou scene of quiet rest,
Where dwells the King Eternal,
Oh, beautiful and blest!
Thy streets are filled with glorious song,
The praises of a myriad throng.

With stones of polished beauty
Is reared thy structure fair;
And gems, and gold, and crystal
Are sparkling everywhere;
With pearls thy gates are glittering gay,
And golden is thy bright highway.

For ever, and in sweetness
Are Alleluias given;
Unending is the feast day,
The royal feast of heaven;
Whate'er within thy walls is stored,
Is pure and holy to the Lord.

No clouds with sombre curtain
Thy glorious brightness screen;
There shines the Sun eternal,
And aye at noonday seen;
There is no night to give repose,
For no one toil or trouble knows.

The vernal glow of spring-time
Is rich and lasting there;
The wealth of summer's beauty
Is scattered everywhere;
And that fair realm can never know
The autumn's blast, or winter's snow.

The notes that fall in sweetness,
Where birds in woodland sing;
The sounds of softest music,
That winds in summer bring,
Are wafted o'er that city bright,
In strains of unalloyed delight.

There youth adorned with vigour
Ne'er into age declines;
No aged fears the mortal,
Nor for the past repines;
For past and future are unknown,
In heaven the present reigns alone.

No fleshly law can triumph,
And over reason ride;
With bodies pure and stainless
The spirit shall abide;
And power of flesh, and power of will,
Shall both one common law fulfil.

Oh, bright the heavenly glory
This fragile frame shall wear,
When health, and strength, and freedom
Shall crown with beauty rare;
And pleasure's draughts no sorrow know,
But everlasting joys bestow.

Now gladly bear the burden;
With zeal thy task maintain;
And gifts shall crown thy labour,
And all thy loss be gain;
When decked with splendour thou shalt be
Where glory shines eternally.

76.

PUGNATE, CHRISTI MILITES

Christian soldiers in the conflict!
Bear the banner of the cross;
Rich reward shall crown the victor,
More than recompense, for loss.

Not with paltry palms that wither
Shall the brow be gaily crowned;
But with light that shines eternal,
And with heavenly joy renowned.

Yours are mansions fair and comely,
There your souls in bliss shall rest;
Stars shall sparkle in their radiance
On the pathway of the blest.

Earthly joys are faint and fleeting,
Earthly favours quickly fade;
Heavenward lift your eyes, expecting
There your true reward is laid.

God be praised, who crowns the victor;
Christ be praised, who saves from sin;
Equal praise to God the Spirit,
By whose aid we fight and win.

77. Refrain

The time is drawing near,
It may not tarry long,
When they who face the conflict here,
Shall join the glorious throng,

Where gladness fills the heart,
And honour crowns the brow;
For tireless service fit me, Lord,
By willing service now.

Let sunshine flood the soul,
When threatening night descends,
That I may see the light serene
No sunset ever ends.

Let strength my spirit nerve,
That, with each labour done,
I may, like those who serve above,
See some new task begun;

The time is drawing near:
Till that bright morning break,
May I, with those who see Thy face,
Thy will, my pleasure make:

Great Collect

Lord, to our humble prayers attend:
Let Thou Thy peace from heaven descend,
And to our souls salvation send.
Have mercy, Lord, upon us.

Rule in our hearts, Thou Prince of Peace,
The welfare of Thy Church increase,
And bid all strife and discord cease.
Have mercy, Lord, upon us.

To all who meet for worship here,
Do Thou in faithfulness draw near;
Inspire with faith and godly fear.
Have mercy, Lord, upon us.

Oh, clothe Thy ministers with might,
To rule within Thy Church aright,
That they may serve as in Thy sight.
Have mercy, Lord, upon us.

The sovereign ruler of our land,
Protect by Thine Almighty hand,
And all around the throne who stand.
Have mercy, Lord, upon us.

Let clouds and sunshine bless the earth,
Give fruits and flowers a timely birth,
Our harvests crown with peaceful mirth,
Have mercy, Lord, upon us.

Let voyages by land and sea
In danger's hour in safety be;
The suffering and the captives free.
Have mercy, Lord, upon us.

Around us let Thy shield be cast,
Till wrath and danger are o'erpast,
And tribulation's bitter blast.
Have mercy, Lord, upon us.

85

79. Harvest

Refrain

Come, praise with gladness the Lord of all creation,
Heaven tells His glory, earth His bounty shews;
Lowly He sought us, and won for us salvation,
Grace fills our lives with goodness He bestows.

Bountiful Giver, Thine be the praise,
Blessing, and honour, and glory, always.

Spring time and harvest, and cloud and summer gladness,
Come to our earth because His promise lives;
Morn smiles with beauty, and evening soothes our sadness--
Such are the treasures that His bounty gives.

Spring time is now, and summer with its beauty;
Brightness and sadness here alternate come;
Lord, may the flowers, and fruits of love and duty,
Blossom and ripen for Thy harvest home.

Then when the angels the reapers at the ending,
Gather the fruitage which our lives have grown,
May we with gladness, angel toil attending,
Sing of the harvest at the heavenly home.

80.

High on the throne of the Ancient of Days,
Lauded by hosts that unceasingly praise,
Christ in the glory He valiantly won,
Reigns in His right, the omnipotent Son.

Highest in rank fall adoringly down,
Cherub, and seraph of peerless renown;
Bowing their heads 'neath the shade of their wings,
Each the Trisagion ceaselessly sings.

Princes and potentates, noble and strong,
They to whom virtue and kin-ship belong,
Lay at His footstool the crowns which they wear,
Honoured to leave them in loyalty there.

Who can approach where such majesty bright,
Fills with its radiance the dwelling of light?
Who, where immortals abide evermore,
Dare in the glory transcendent adore?

Lo, from the regions of sorrow they come,
Singing, whose lips in the darkness were dumb;
Thousands, ten thousands, with offerings of love,
Rise to the bliss that receives them above.

Thou hast redeemed them, O Christ, they are Thine,
Pure as the hosts in Thy presence they shine;
They with the angels adoringly praise,
Blending their song with immortals' always.

81.

Ah, that blest abode above,
Who shall pass its portals?
Who at length in peace and love,
Dwell with the immortals?

They who battle for the right
When the day is longest;
They who conquer in the fight,
When the foe is strongest.

Who shall, nearest to the throne,
Have a place appointed?
Who have greatest favour shewn
By the Lord's Anointed?

They who serve Him gladly now,
King and Captain royal;
Ever mindful of their vow,
Noble, steadfast, loyal.

Ah, the bliss of heaven's abode:
Rise, my soul, to win it!
Shrink not from the weary road,
But in faith begin it.

List not to the call of sense,
Earth is vain and lying;
Yonder is thy recompense,
'Mid a bliss undying.

Forward ever, day by day,
Tread the path of duty;
Angels help you in the way
To the realm of beauty.

82.

I sought the Lord at early morn,
When earth awoke to see the light;
And to my soul a light was borne
That quelled the darkness of my night;
He heard my prayer at early morn,
And light into my heart was borne.

I sought the Lord when noontide shone,
And head and hand earth's duties shared;
"I am Thy servant, Lord, alone,"
I said, and told Him how I fared;
He heard my prayer as I drew near,
And kept me at my task, sincere.

I sought the Lord when evening fell,
And night came gliding on apace;
For I had sins my Lord to tell,
And He is full of pardoning grace;
He heard my prayer, and bade me rest,
And in His love my soul was blest.

At morn, at noon, at night, I'll pray,
And Thou, O Lord, my prayer wilt hear;
For Thou art near my path alway,
To aid, to comfort, or to cheer;
No hour too early, none too late,
To knock imploring at Thy gate.

O Jesus Christ, to Thee be praise!
'Tis Thou hast taught my soul to pray,
For Thou didst speak with God always,
At morn, at noon, at close of day;
And Thou hast said He hears the prayer
The longing soul breathes everywhere.

83.

Let a shining robe be mine,
Spotless as the snow drift white,
Thou, who for Thy form Divine,
Mak'st a garment of the light.

Darkness from Thy presence flies,
Thou art light: and where Thou art,
Radiance, as from heavenly skies,
Seeks, effulgent, every heart.

Far I wandered from the right,
Dark around, and dark within;
Groping in the gloom of night,
Wounded in the ways of sin.

And my rags with mire defiled,
Clothe my naked soul with shame;
For, from Thee, a wayward child,
I have wandered to my blame.

Let Thy presence fill my soul,
Let my heart Thy nearness feel;
Speak the word, and I am whole;
Touch my wounds, and they shall heal.

Then the night that round me lies,
At Thy presence shall depart;
And a glorious light arise
In the darkness of my heart.

Let a shining robe be mine,
Spotless as the snow drift white;
Thou, who, for Thy form Divine,
Mak'st a garment of the light.

84.

I am alone, yet not alone,
For Thou art near:
I cannot see Thy loving face,
But I can hear
The cheering promise of Thy grace.

Thou wilt not leave me in the dark
When falls the night;
For round my path and in my soul
Thou art the Light
To guide me with Thy sweet control.

No want can steal my rich supplies
Of love and peace;
For though I lack what others hold,
My stores increase
With heavenly gifts more rare than gold.

And Thou wilt bear me all life through,
And in the end
Wilt still abide what Thou hast been,
My constant Friend,
And take me where Thy face is seen.

85.

Oh, the Cross, the Saviour dying,
Wounded sore, and faint, and sighing,
Bowed beneath the burden lying
On His spotless soul.

'Tis thy load He falters under;
Speaks not heaven in wrathful thunder?
Earth! behold the sight, and wonder,
Love has borne the rod.

Canst thou love the sin that bound Him,
Threw the robe of scorn around Him,
Mocking bowed the knee, and crowned Him
With the cruel thorn?

Jesus, at Thy feet relenting,
Bring I all my guilt repenting,
All my cruel sin lamenting:
Christ, my sin forgive!

86.

I wandered sore distressed,
All weary and forlorn;
I had no place to rest,
Of all my pleasures shorn--
My thirsting spirit sighed,
And in the desert cried.

The Shepherd heard my cry,
Who came His flock to find,
And drew in mercy nigh,
For He is wondrous kind;
His winning voice awoke
My spirit as He spoke.

He bade my wandering cease,
And gave my heart a home,
That, from the bliss of peace,
I might no longer roam;
He gave me hope for fears,
And lasting joy for tears.

87.

Once the Lord, for our salvation,
Left the realm of endless bliss;
And to serve, in lowly station,
Came to such a world as this.

Weary oft He toiled in weakness,
Winning erring lives from wrong;
Dwelling with the poor in meekness,
Bidding fainting souls be strong;

Bearing scorn and rude deriding,
From the proud who passed Him by;
Never the repentant chiding
For their guilt and misery.

For His heart with love o'erflowing,
Bound Him to our needy race;
Day by day the gifts bestowing
From the fulness of His grace.

Once upon a cross uplifted,
Did the Lord for sinners die,
That there might to man be gifted,
Life, to live eternally.

Shall I then with such a Giver,
Claim whate'er I have as mine?
Nay, myself and mine, for ever,
To His service I resign.

88.

Close beside the heart that loves me
Would I rest in sorrow's hour,
With a Father's smile above me,
And beneath--an arm of power.

Weak and worthless, worn and weary,
Welcome bids my faith be strong;
Sorrow's hour is short, if dreary,
Joy shall last through ages long.

Dark the hour, but comes the morrow,
Dawn shall waken by and by;
Light shall gild the clouds of sorrow
When the sun is in the sky.

Rest, my soul: that love unfailing
Strengthens in the hour of woe--
For the pain thy life assailing
Found Him when He dwelt below.

89.

My soul doth wait on God,
From Him my help proceeds;
His mercy is exceeding broad,
To overtake my needs.

He gives His pardoning grace,
When I my sin confess;
Nor ever hides from me His face
In my distressfulness.

The Spirit of all power,
Most freely He bestows;
And I am strong in evil hour,
When pressed by direst foes.

Oh, He has gifts in store,
More rich than wealth commands;
And when His pity I implore,
He fills my empty hands.

God, Thou art good and kind,
And full of tender grace;
Have me for ever in Thy mind,
Nor hide from me Thy face.

90.

The chariots of the Lord are strong,
Their number passeth ken;
Mount them and fight against the wrong,
Ye who are valiant men.

Where, unabashed, the power of sin
Vaunts an unhindered sway,
Ride, in the strength of God, and win
Fresh laurels in the fray.

For freedom wield the sword of might,
And cut the bands that bind;
Strike boldly in the cause of right,
And still fresh laurels find.

Where hands are weak, and hearts are faint,
Through conflict sharp and sore;
Where hearts that murmur no complaint,
Shrink at the thought of more:

There let the power of God be shown,
To quell satanic might;
To rescue those who strive alone,
Despondent in the fight.

Ride on, the chariots of the Lord,
Dispel the hosts of sin;
Ye who are valiant, wield the sword,
And still fresh laurels win.

91.

O heavenly land beyond the sun!
Far away;
Where pilgrims rest, their wanderings done,
Far away;
Where sin and sorrow, grief and pain,
Shall ne'er afflict the soul again,
Far away.

O heavenly land of promise sweet!
Far away;
Where Christ and His redeemed shall meet,
Far away;
Where love and peace shall fill the heart,
And joy respond in every part,
Far away.

O blessed land where Jesus is!
Far away;
Where all shall come He claims as His
Far away;
The pure in heart, the meek, are there,
And oh, that land is passing fair!
Far away.

O blessed land beyond the sun!
Far away;
I'll share thy joys when earth is done,
Far away;
Lord Jesus, fit me by Thy grace,
And in Thy love prepare a place,
Far away.

92.

There is no friend like Jesus,
So constant and so kind;
He heals the wounded spirit,
And calms the troubled mind.

The hungry soul He feedeth
With manna from His store;
And of His living water
We drink to thirst no more.

When weary is our journey,
And heavy is our load,
This constant Friend is with us,
To cheer our toilsome road.

When bright our path and joyous,
And sunshine floods the way,
Our joy He renders tenfold
More joyous every day.

There is no friend like Jesus,
So constant is His love;
The earth has seen His kindness,
'Twill be enjoyed above.

Through death's dark vale He'll lead us--
That vale He passed before;
With life immortal clothe us,
To be unclothed no more.

And in that land the fairest,
With joys that never end,
Our Lord shall stand supremely,
Our true and constant Friend.

93.

When I heard the Saviour calling
Weary, burdened souls to rest--
"'Tis the voice of love that calleth,
I will honour His behest;"
And I found repose from sorrow,
Leaning on my Saviour's breast.

Weary souls, all upward toiling,
Have ye sorrow for your care?
Wherefore bend beneath the burden
Which your Lord will gladly share?
He can bear your weight of sorrow,
Who the cross to Calvary bare.

Seek not rest in worldly promise;
Worldly rest hath troubled dreams;
Not so true the world's fulfilment,
As at first the promise seems.
He who tastes the Living Water
Thirsts not after other streams.

Hear the voice of Jesus calling,
Take the burden He bestows,
'Tis a load, the more you bear it,
Lighter and yet lighter grows;
And at length the faithful bearer
Finds an undisturbed repose.

94.

I would not have a hand to guide
But Thine;
For Thou hast trod where sinners stray,
And knowest well life's troubled way,
And mine.

I would not have a will to rule
But Thine;
For Thou art wise as Thou art good,
And none can better choose what should
Be mine.

Oh, I would tread the sorest path
For Thee;
For Thou canst make the roughest plain,
Give joy for grief, and calm the pain
For me.

95.

O Jesus, let me hear Thy voice,
No music sweeter to my ear;
It tells my drooping heart to hope,
For Thou art near.

Speak when the tempest fiercely blows,
Bid Thou its angry raging cease;
For where Thy voice is heard, there reigns
Eternal peace.

Speak when the clouds in dusky folds
Hide from mine eyes the noontide sun;
For when Thy voice proclaims Thy will,
Thy will is done.

O Jesus, let Thy voice be heard
In stilly eve and buoyant morn;
And let the peace it brings, each day
My life adorn.

96.

Come, rest awhile; 'tis eventide--
The hour to meditation dear;
And set the cares of life aside,
For God is near.

Oh, let a thankful spirit tell
The wonders of His heavenly grace,
The love that loves us, all too well,
Who spurn His grace.

Amid our daily life He bears
Our cold despite and thankless scorn;
As if He gave not rest at eve,
And joy at morn.

Thou gav'st me, Lord, at early morn,
A gift unsullied, for my care;
Another day, I might adorn
With graces rare.

I dare not tell it to my God
But oh, that gift's no longer bright;
He gave it with the charm of morn,
And now 'tis night.

O God, 'tis well at eventide,
The hour for meditation given,
To know we're welcome at Thy side--
Foretaste of heaven.

For oh, one precious day misspent,
Is all too great a load to bear;
But I will lay it at Thy feet,
And leave it there.

97.

We bless Thee, Lord, that Thou hast spread
A table for Thy people here;
Where we may taste the Living Bread,
And feel Thy blessed presence near.

Here, where Thy people meet, Thou art;
We hear Thy voice in accents sweet;
Thy blood is wine to fainting heart,
Thy flesh to hungry spirits meat.

Oh, help us, Lord, to feast with joy
Upon the bounties of Thy grace;
Here may no anxious thoughts annoy,
Here may we see Thy loving face.

O Christ, who, in Thy love untold,
Didst give Thyself to death for man,
Here at Thy table, Lord, unfold
The beauty of Redemption's plan.

Oh, send Thy Spirit to our aid--
That Spirit promised long ago,
When first the solemn feast was laid,
Even in the valley of Thy woe.

And let Him bring sweet comfort near,
And when we see the thorn-decked brow,
We may remember He who died
Is crowned with life immortal now.

98.

Hark the voice of angels.
Listen to their praise;
Christ the Lord of glory
Is their song always;
Never are they weary,
Ever do they sing,
For they dwell in Zion,
And they love its King.
Hark! they tell the glory
Of the heavenly King;
Glad their hearts to serve Him,
Glad the praise they bring.

Hark! the voice of children,
In the heavenly throng;
And they praise the Saviour,
With a sweeter song;
For He died to save them,
In His matchless love,
And rejoicing brought them
To His home above.
Hark! they tell the wonders
Of redeeming grace;
Dwelling in the sunshine
Of the Saviour's face.

Hark! the voice of children,
Singing here below--
Pilgrims on a journey,
Up to Zion we go;
Faint our youthful praises,
Sweeter yet we'll sing,
When we reach the palace
Of the heavenly King.
Hark! the voice of children,
Singing here below--
Pilgrims on a journey,
Up to Zion we go.

Hail the smile of morning!
Hills and valleys sing,
Sunlight is adorning
Every pleasant thing;

Not a note of sadness
Mars the tuneful lay;
Melody of gladness
Greets the coming day.
Lend your gleeful voices,
Children, to the lay;
Morn of life rejoices,
As the morn of day.

Love is like the morning,
Smiling from the hills;
All our life adorning,
Banishing our ills;
In the love that greets us,
Every opening day,
God our Father meets us,
Smiling on our way.
Let our hearts adoring,
God of love adore;
Aye His grace imploring
That we love Him more.

99.

O, come in early morning,
The Saviour's heart is kind;
And they who seek Him early,
Are ever sure to find;
They cannot miss the pathway,
When all around is bright;
They lose the path and stumble,
Who tarry till the night.

Oh, come in early morning,
The dew is on the flower,
There's laughter in the woodland,
And music in the bower;
The world is full of gladness,
And sings the Maker's praise,
There's not a note of sadness,
To mar the matin lays.

Oh, come in early morning,
The sun is climbing high;
And all the world is smiling,
Beneath a cloudless sky;
There's not a piping blackbird,
But sings with lusty glee;
There's not a little lambkin,
But frolics on the lea.

Oh, come in early morning,
It cannot aye be bright,
The night shall fold its curtains,
And hide the joyous light;
And gloom, and grief, and sadness,
Shall be in every song;
Oh, come in early morning,
And serve Him all day long.

Oh, come in early morning,
Oh, come with laughing eye,
Oh, come with pulses bounding,
And hope that's soaring high;

Hymns of the Early Church
The joy of morn shall linger
Throughout a joyous day,
And in the night the gladness
No gloom shall chase away.

www.ingramcontent.com/pod-product-compliance
Lightning Source LLC
Chambersburg PA
CBHW032007080426
42735CB00007B/535